S P R I N G

SPRING

Ron Hirschi

Photographs by

Thomas D. Mangelsen

A WILDLIFE SEASONS BOOK

SCHOLASTIC INC.

New York Toronto London Auckland Sydney

Text copyright © 1990 by Ron Hirschi.
Photographs copyright © 1990 by Thomas D. Mangelsen.
All rights reserved. Published by Scholastic Inc.,
730 Broadway, New York, NY 10003, by arrangement with
Cobblehill Books, an affiliate of Dutton Children's Books, a division of
Penguin Books USA Inc.
Printed in the U.S.A.
ISBN 0-590-46077-3

        3 4 5 6 7 8 9 10   08   99 98 97 96 95 94 93

To Shannon and Shae
R.H.

To my brother Bill
and his children,
Mary, Paul, Annie,
Jennifer, and Michael
T.M.

Spring hides
beneath the winter snow.
Spring waits.
Then one day
lilies, daisies,
and shooting star
flowers pop up.

Yellow fawn lily

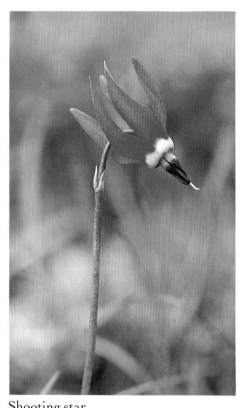

Shooting star

Waking
like mother bear
and her cub from a
long winter nap…

Grizzly sow and cub in the snow

the wildflowers march
up the mountainside.

As the snow melts
away, weasels change
from winter white
to golden brown.

Long-tailed weasel

Trumpeter swan

Now, swans search for a safe place
to build a nest,
while coyotes and mountain sheep
shed their thick winter coats.

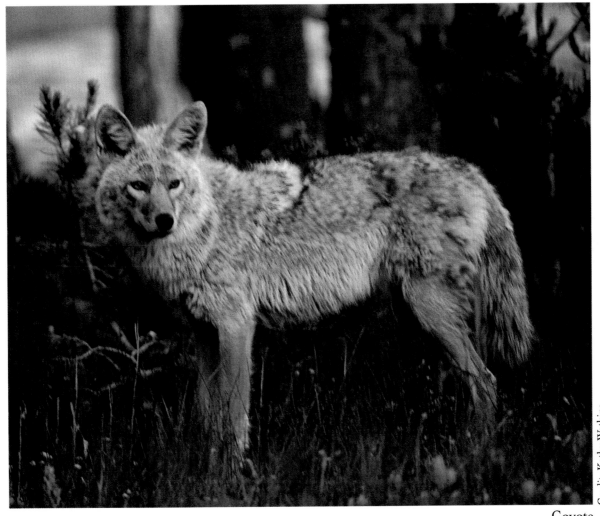

Coyote

Credit: Kathy Watkins

Spring is time for
baby owls to grow
bigger each day.
They wait for mother
owl to return with
a fat mouse.

Great horned owl and owlets
Credit: Kathy Watkins

She hunts where cottontails hide and where goldfinches dot the fields like flowers in the sun.

Snowshoe hare

Goldfinch

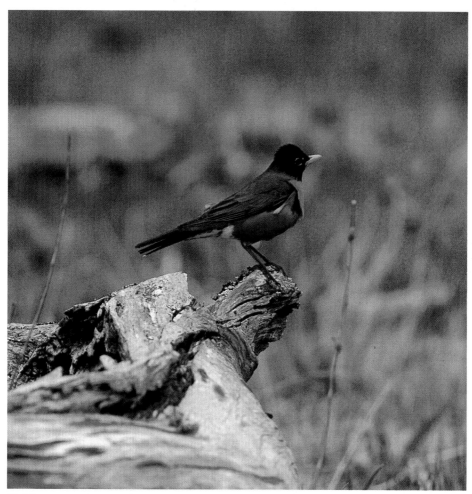
Robin

Spring is a
robin's morning song
that seems to last
all day long.

It is time for marmots to scurry from their burrows.

Marmot

They sit in the first warm spring sun, while woodpeckers and wrens choose snug nesting holes.

Woodpecker

House wren

Willow ptarmigan

Ptarmigan search
for just the right place
to raise a family too
—high in the hills
where baby elk
are born...

where the bluebird
sings its mountain
song.

Mountain bluebird

Elk

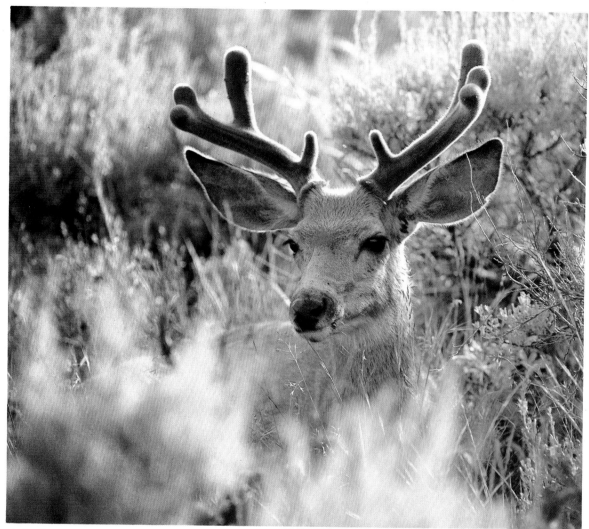

Mule deer

Spring is time
for antlers to grow,
hummingbirds to
suddenly appear,

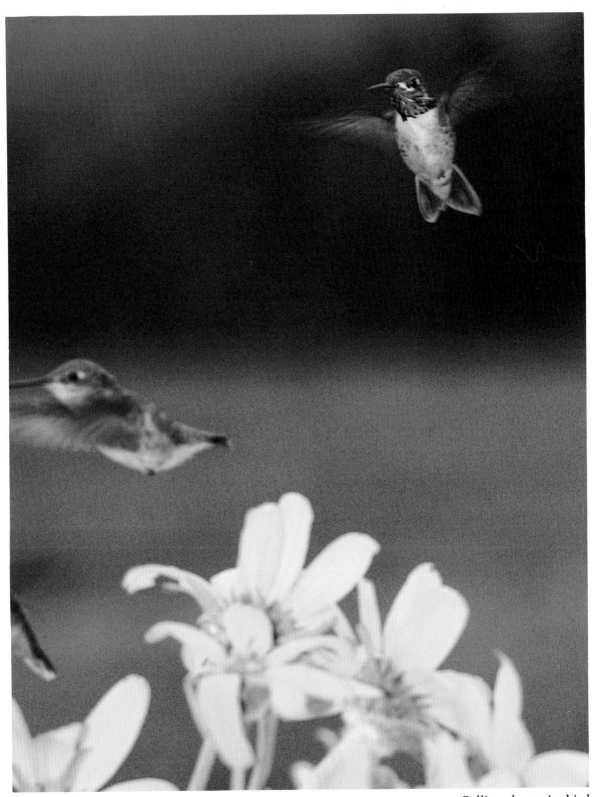

Calliope hummingbird

and baby geese to pop
into their new world.

Canada gosling and eggs

Spring is time
for young and old to
begin a new year.

Moose cow and calf

Bison with calf

Summer
will soon
be here.

AFTERWORD

Spring can be the best of times for plants and animals. It is the season of birth. It is the season of new growth. Warmth due to longer days and relief from cold winter snow is welcomed by bird song and arrival of migratory animals from their wintering grounds. Bears burst from hibernation dens. Marmots whistle once again in the highlands. Hummingbirds magically appear as soon as the first red flowers blossom.

Many animals now change their feathers or fur coats to fit into the landscape or to fit into the needs of the season. Weasels and ptarmigan turn from white to brown. Coyotes and other animals that do not migrate south in winter now shed to a lighter layer of fur. And, the songbirds put on a dazzling display of brightly colored feathers. Goldfinches, warblers, and bluebirds are among the most beautiful. Even the robin is much more brightly colored now than in other seasons.

It is no surprise that so many changes happen in harmony during the first weeks of spring. Flowers blossom. Insects emerge. Leaves uncurl from their winter buds. All these provide colorful displays for our eyes. They also provide an abundance of food for deer, rabbits, bears, and other wild animals. That abundant new supply of food stimulates growth and offers a chance for animals to begin to raise a family. Now is a great time for you to help too; a properly placed birdhouse will give you a chance to watch a family of swallows, wrens, or bluebirds make a new spring beginning. Their songs will last all summer long.